Wife After Death

A Comedy

Eric Chappell

A SAMUEL FRENCH ACTING EDITION

SAMUEL FRENCH

FOUNDED 1830

SAMUELFRENCH.COM
SAMUELFRENCH-LONDON.CO.UK

ISBN 978-0-573-11475-5

www.SamuelFrench.com
www.SamuelFrench-London.co.uk

FOR PRODUCTION ENQUIRIES

UNITED STATES AND CANADA
Info@SamuelFrench.com
1-866-598-8449

UNITED KINGDOM AND EUROPE
Theatre@SamuelFrench-London.co.uk
020-7255-4302

Each title is subject to availability from Samuel French, depending upon country of performance. Please be aware that WIFE AFTER DEATH may not be licensed by Samuel French in your territory. Professional and amateur producers should contact the nearest Samuel French office or licensing partner to verify availability.

WIFE AFTER DEATH

First presented on 17th March 2010 at the Theatre
Royal, Brighton, with the following cast:

Harvey Barrett Mel	Tom Conti
Vi Barrett Sharon	Diane Fletcher
Kevin Prewitt Ian	Royce Mills
Jane Prewitt Kate	Diana Marchment
Kay Lauren	Elizabeth Payne
Laura Thursby Jane	Nina Young

Directed by Tom Conti and Tom Kinninmont
Designed by Norman Coates
Lighting design by Leonard Tucker

CHARACTERS

Jan Fox **Laura Thursby**, 40s. Widow. Attractive, dressed in fashionable black, vain about her appearance.

Sharon **Vi Barrett,** older than Laura with a fuller figure and dressed in simple black. She has a wry attitude to the events being played out in front of her.

Mel **Harvey Barrett,** 50s. Untidy, angry man. His only concession to the day is a crumpled black tie.

Ian **Kevin Prewitt,** 30s. A slim, pale man in a dark suit and dark glasses. Handkerchief in hand — much moved.

Kate **Jane Prewitt,** 30s. Thin and gawky, inclined to be flustered.

Lauren **Kay,** 50s. Trim figure, tight dress. A smoker with a sardonic manner.

SYNOPSIS OF SCENES

The action of the play takes place in Laura Thursby's spacious sitting-room.

ACT I An afternoon in summer
ACT II Three weeks later

Time — the present

Other plays by Eric Chappell
published by Samuel French Ltd:

Cut and Dried
Double Vision
Father's Day
Fiddlers Three (comprising Cut and Dried
and We Don't Want To Lose You)
Haunted
Haywire
Heatstroke
It Can Damage Your Health
Natural Causes
Rising Damp
Something's Burning
Summer End
Theft
Up and Coming
We Don't Want To Lose You

ACT I

Laura Thursby's spacious sitting-room overlooking a garden. One afternoon in summer

A door, R, *leads to the hall.* UL *are french windows open to the terrace and garden. The curtains are half drawn. There is a desk, sofa and chairs, a bin and a sideboard with a drinks tray with drinks and glasses on it. An open coffin rests on a stand in the far corner of the room,* UR. *It is lit by a single spotlight. Faintly from the hall is the sound of the song "Getting to Know You" from "The King and I"*

Voices off. Laura Thursby leads the way into the room from the hall. She is about 40, attractive and dressed entirely in fashionable black with a hat and veil. She is followed by Vi and Harvey Barrett. Vi is a little older than Laura with a fuller figure. She is wearing a simple black dress and jacket. Harvey, 50s, is dressed more casually but wears a black tie. They turn towards Laura who throws back her veil

Laura (*softly*) I'll leave you here for a few moments ...
Vi (*reverently*) Yes, we'd like that.
Laura I know you'd want to ...
Vi Yes.
Laura Be alone with ...
Vi Of course ...
Laura And possibly ... (*She gestures to the coffin*)

Laura moves out through the french windows waving to someone in the garden

Harvey (*frowning*) Possibly what?
Vi See him.
Harvey I don't want to see him.
Vi Why not? He was your best friend.
Harvey He's a dead body now. I prefer to remember him as he was.

Vi crosses and looks into the coffin

Vi He hasn't changed much.

Harvey What do you mean — he hasn't changed much? He's dead. You can't change more than that.

Vi Not really. (*After a pause*) I think Laura would like you to pay your respects.

Harvey You pay your respects. I was his closest friend — and I can tell you, he'd have hated this. (*He crosses to the drinks tray and pours himself a drink*)

Vi Well, of course, he'd have hated this. You don't have to be his closest friend to know that. He's in a box. Given the choice he'd prefer to be standing where you are.

Harvey He'd have hated this display.

Vi He was a public figure.

Harvey That has nothing to do with it. He had taste. This is vulgar ceremonial. If she had to have the coffin here — the lid should have been screwed firmly down. It's morbid. It's in bad taste. Did you see the size of that veil? She could be chewing it with the sandwiches if she's not careful. What a production.

Vi You think it's a production?

Harvey The grieving widow. She should be on a road safety poster. And I'll tell you this — that veil's not to hide eyes red from weeping. If Dave was here —

Vi Dave is here.

Harvey What?

Vi Harve, he's in that coffin.

Harvey I keep forgetting. He was like a brother to me, Vi. I can't get used to it.

Vi (*sympathetically*) I know. Perhaps if you saw him …

Harvey I'll need another drink. I'm as dry as a ship's biscuit.

Vi Not too much — remember what happened to Dave.

Harvey He should have been in a chapel of rest. He'd have preferred that. It's not as if he was happy here. That's the trouble with death — you're left out of the decision making. He should have left instructions in his will.

Vi He didn't make a will. Laura thought it's what he'd have wanted.

Harvey No — it's what she wanted. His theme song's playing in the hall — he's under a spotlight which on a day like this could hasten decomposition. (*He switches off the light*) And outside there's a hearse that's all glass with four black plumed horses. They'll think we're burying Dracula.

Vi Laura thought it needed something special. David always loved show. She tried to get an old fire engine.

Harvey A fire engine! My God!

They listen to the music

Just listen. I half expect him to walk in in his blue tuxedo.
Vi He's wearing his blue tuxedo.
Harvey (*squeamishly*) Is he?
Vi Are you sure you don't want to —— ?
Harvey No. She's enjoying this.
Vi No.
Harvey She's having a good time.
Vi What do you want her to do? Go around screeching and tearing her hair out in handfuls? You'd have hated that.

Harvey stares out of the window

Harvey I'd like some genuine feeling ...

Vi goes down on her knees by the coffin and prays. Harvey turns and stares in surprise

Are you praying?
Vi Yes.
Harvey You don't believe in it.
Vi Better to be on the safe side — for Dave's sake.
Harvey Dave didn't believe in it. He told me once — he only believed in two things — love and laughter ... (*He turns away emotionally*) Not a bad philosophy. Not that he got much of it here.
Vi I think they were happy in their own way.
Harvey Then it was a very strange way. If he was happy why did he kill himself?
Vi He didn't. It was a stroke — he drank too much.
Harvey When a man drinks too much — look at the wife.
Vi You drink too much.

Harvey drinks deeply

Harvey I'm cutting back.
Vi Everyone's cutting back, now.
Harvey Why do we have to stay here? (*He peers out*) Where is she?
Vi At the end of the drive. She's frightened people might miss the house.
Harvey She should have tied balloons to the gate.
Vi Harvey.
Harvey Black ones.

Vi It's still not funny.

Harvey I've got it. "I knew the widow wasn't exactly grief-stricken when she tied balloons to the gate on the day of the funeral." We could use that.

Vi Harve, you're not writing for Dave now.

Harvey (*sadly*) No.

Vi You don't think she's grieving?

Harvey You saw that outfit — must have cost a fortune.

Vi It's her way of coping.

Harvey Then she's coping very well.

Vi It's a tribute to Dave.

Harvey It's a tribute to her figure. Did you see her contours? You don't expect to see contours on a widow — not on the day of the funeral. She's already looking around. Probably already written out the ad. "Fun-loving widow — good standard of health — non-smoker — Surrey and parts of Middlesex — prepared to go further."

Vi Harvey, stop it — someone might hear you.

Harvey It puts me in mind of that Oscar Wilde line. "Her hair turned quite gold from grief." (*He studies Vi*) Well thank God, you're sensibly dressed.

Vi I'm not sure I want to be sensibly dressed.

Harvey At least you didn't go out and buy something like that.

Vi I couldn't get into something like that. I wore this at your father's funeral — and your mother's. I knew it would come in handy. It pays to have something black in the wardrobe at our time of life. You never know who's going to be next.

Harvey Well, don't look at me.

Vi (*smiling*) My mother always said, "You can't go wrong in a little black dress." — And I always said, "But I want to go wrong, Mother." But she never got it.

Harvey That's because it's a lousy joke. And you'd stand more chance of going wrong if you lost weight.

Vi Does it show?

Harvey Yes.

Vi I'm going on a diet.

Harvey Everyone's going on a diet since Dave went. (*He looks out of the window again*) Quite a crowd. The church is going to be full.

Vi Yes. Ken and Jimmy are here.

Harvey (*pleased*) Are they? I knew they'd come. Shows the esteem in which he was held. (*Gloomily*) I don't suppose they'd come to mine.

Vi You don't think so?

Harvey No. I wouldn't get a crowd like this. (*Pause*) In fact, I don't suppose I'd get anyone.

Vi I'd come.
Harvey Of course you'd come! You're my wife.
Vi And then there's the children.
Harvey Of course there's the children.
Vi Although I'm not too sure about Paul.
Harvey (*staring*) You're not?
Vi Not too sure.
Harvey Why not?
Vi He hates funerals.
Harvey Oh.
Vi Your parents would have come — if they'd been alive.
Harvey I know that! What about your parents?
Vi Doubtful.
Harvey Is it?
Vi They've never cared for you.
Harvey Why?
Vi They don't like your sense of humour.
Harvey What! Don't they realize I earn my living by it?
Vi Yes. They still don't like it.
Harvey You may have noticed we haven't mentioned any friends.
Vi You haven't got any friends. Not now. You spent all your time with Dave.
Harvey I don't have any friends because you don't entertain. Dave was my closest friend and he never came to my house — he never came to dinner. Why?
Vi He didn't want to come to dinner. I asked him.
Harvey It was the way you asked him. You didn't want him to come to dinner. You hate entertaining.
Vi All right. Now Dave's gone I'll entertain and you'll have friends.

Harvey becomes thoughtful

Harvey That gives me an idea — for the opening. (*He takes some notes from his pocket*)
Vi Opening of what?
Harvey My valediction. Gives me a funny opening ...
Vi (*uneasily*) It's not going to be too funny ...?
Harvey (*staring*) Laura said keep it light.
Vi But not too light.
Harvey (*frowning*) No. (*He clears his throat*) I'd like to talk today about the man who was Thursby ——
Vi Why do you say it like that?

Harvey Like what?

Vi The man who was Thursby? It sounds strange.

Harvey It's a literary reference. (*Pause*) G. K. Chesterton. (*Pause*) *The Man Who Was Thursday.*

Vi But he's Thursby.

Harvey I know that!

Vi They won't get it.

Harvey I thought you might. Every so often I see a glimmer of intelligence behind that blank stare and I get hopeful. I get the same feeling from your parents.

Vi They still won't get it.

Harvey scores the line out

What's the funny opening?

Harvey (*clearing his throat*) I want to talk about one of the nicest men I've known. (*Pause*) Mind you, I don't know many people. (*He pauses, beaming in anticipation of a laugh*)

Vi That's not funny.

Harvey Dave would have laughed.

Vi Harvey, the only person who would have laughed isn't going to join in.

Harvey All right. (*Pause*) The last time Dave died was at the Glasgow Empire — he told me he didn't enjoy the experience that much ...

Vi shakes her head. Harvey's voice dies away

... No?

Vi No.

Harvey crumples the sheet and drops it into the bin

Is there going to be much more like that?

Harvey (*frowning*) No.

Vi Aren't you going to mention his awards — and his work for charity?

Harvey Yes, of course. (*Grinning*) And that time when he was legless and he went skidding round that field at the pro-am — and ran into my car ...

Vi shakes her head

... No?

Crumple   & throw

Harvey crumples another sheet of paper and drops it into the bin

Vi Just concentrate on the good works, Harve. (*She glances at the door*)
She'll be back in a minute. Don't you think you should ...? She'll
ask.   *Has a drink*

*Harvey sighs and downs his drink. He takes a deep breath, crosses to
the coffin and looks in*

Well? What do you think?

Harvey He looks pissed off.

Vi Well, of course he does — he's in a coffin. But apart from that?

Harvey There's no apart from that. (*He turns away*) He would have
started the new series today. I'd finished the scripts on time for once.
When you were down on your knees just now did you ask God why?
Why Dave?

Vi No.

Harvey No, I suppose you were frightened of offending him.

Vi Well, yes ...

Harvey (*shaking his head*) You don't believe He exists but you're
frightened of offending Him. It's a good question though, isn't it?
Why Dave? When all those bastards are still walking about.

Vi What bastards?

Harvey The world's full of bastards. And most of them work in
television. Why Dave and not one of them? Why not the Programme
Controller? That would have raised a cheer. Why not Head of Light
Entertainment — he wouldn't see a joke, except by appointment —
then he'd be late. I would have even settled for our producer — he
wouldn't have been missed. But it had to be Dave — and all he ever
did was make people laugh. And all they ever did was live off him.

Vi They could say that about you.

Harvey I never lived off Dave. (*Proudly*) I was a member of the talent.
I helped him reach the heights. When I first met him he was living
in a shoebox in Earls Court. The day he died he owned two houses
and a villa in Portugal. I just hope he enjoyed them. (*He turns away
emotionally*)

Vi (*quietly*) I suppose it was written.

Harvey (*turning back; passionately*) You suppose it was written! You're
not a Moslem, are you?

Laura enters from the hall

*Harvey turns away again. Laura regards Harvey's back. Laura and Vi
exchange glances*

Laura Is he, er ...?
Vi A little but I think it's better that ...
Laura That's what I thought. Once he's ...
Vi Then he can ...
Laura Begin to ...

Harvey turns sharply

Harvey Are you two ever going to finish a sentence?
Laura What did you think of him, Harvey?
Harvey I thought he looked ... (*Glancing at Vi*) ... Peaceful ...
Laura Yes, I thought so. After the strain of the last few weeks he found
rest.
Harvey I think he'd have preferred the strain.
Laura Did you notice he was wearing his blue tuxedo — the lucky
one?
Harvey Yes, it did catch my eye.
Laura I've tried to think of everything.
Vi And you do have a lovely day for it.
Laura Yes. It's as if all nature knows when a good man dies. Although
it must be hard to leave the world on a day like this, Vi.
Harvey I think the day he actually left it was pittling down.
Vi Harvey ...
Laura No, Harvey's right. He's already left us. He's not really in that
coffin.
Harvey He was when I looked.
Laura He's somewhere else now.
Vi At least you were happy, Laura. You've nothing to regret. He loved
you.
Laura (*smiling*) I know. But there is something to regret.
Vi What's that?
Laura He never really believed that I loved him.
Vi Of course he did.
Laura No, he always doubted me. He once said, "Why did a beautiful
woman like you marry someone like me?"
Harvey (*incredulously*) He said that?
Laura Yes. "Why did you marry someone as ugly as me?"
Harvey He wasn't ugly.
Laura I know, but he was insecure. He felt ugly. He was so jealous. You
know how jealous he could be, Harvey.

Harvey No.

Laura He always thought there was someone else. He'd become so passionate. His intensity frightened me sometimes — his depth of feeling. I never knew how to respond.

Vi I'm sure you did. I know you made him happy, Laura.

Harvey stares at Vi in disbelief

Laura I tried. God knows, I tried. On the morning of the day it happened I was leaving the house first. I kissed him lightly on the cheek and walked to the car when some instinct made me turn back and kiss him again, on the lips. He looked surprised. I smiled. He died shortly afterwards.

Vi With your kiss on his lips.

Laura Yes. Could you mention that in your address, Harve — or do you think it's too sentimental?

Harvey I think it's ——

Vi I'm sure he can.

Laura You'll speak first, Harvey — after the first hymn.

Harvey (*suspiciously*) Who's speaking second?

Laura Kevin.

Harvey Kevin?

Laura Well, after your light-hearted piece we thought we'd finish on a more serious note. Now I'd better return to my guests. Don't feel you have to ... I just thought ...

Vi You were absolutely ...

Laura Because you were his ...

Vi Yes ...

Laura and Vi embrace. Laura proffers her cheek; Vi kisses it. Harvey frowns. Laura goes to the door then pauses

Laura Oh, and Harve. No jokes about his meanness. I know it was a running gag in the show but I don't think it's the right time, do you?

Laura exits

Harvey glares after Laura for a moment then takes another sheet from his notes and throws it into the bin

Harvey After death the next casualty is truth. He was mean. If he paid you a compliment, he'd want a receipt for it. But he wasn't mean in the big things. When he ran into my car he wanted to buy me a new one. That's the sort of man he was.

Vi She means well.

Harvey Does she? Do you know something? Grief doesn't change people. They remain the same shites they've always been. She was only here a minute and she managed to pay herself a compliment. "Why did a beautiful woman like you marry someone like me?" He wasn't jealous. Oh, there was someone else she was keen on but he knew who it was.

Vi Who?

Harvey Her! She's always loved herself.

Laura Still, I think it was nice that she kissed him on the lips.

Harvey The shock probably killed him. He's been getting the cheek turned for years. (*He demonstrates*) "Lips that have touched liquor shall never touch mine." No one gets near those sacred lips.

Vi Why — have you tried?

Harvey No, thank you. The kiss of the Black Widow spider is invariably fatal ... (*He crosses to the window and looks out. He smiles mysteriously*) Mind you, she was right in a way ... There was someone else.

Vi What do you mean?

Harvey Dave was having an affair.

Vi You're joking.

Harvey No.

Vi I don't believe it. The press would have got hold of it.

Harvey I was the only one who knew — the only one he trusted. He knew I wouldn't talk.

Vi You're talking now.

Harvey He's dead.

Vi Who was it?

Harvey He didn't tell me that.

Vi So he didn't trust you that much.

Harvey I didn't ask. If he'd wanted to tell me — he'd have told me. That's what friends are for. All he'd say was, "If Laura asks, we were working late tonight." — Then he'd wink.

Vi Wink? And that was it?

Harvey Yes.

Vi So when you said you were working late with Dave — you weren't?

Harvey No.

Vi Where were you?

Harvey (*frowning*) Working.

Vi Or in the bar?

Harvey Yes — why not?

Vi And while you were in the bar he was seeing someone?
Harvey Yes.
Vi But you don't know who it was?
Harvey I do. I worked it out. I'm looking at her now ... (*He waves to someone through the window*)

Vi follows his gaze

Vi You don't mean?
Harvey Yes.
Vi I can hardly believe it. Poor Kevin.
Harvey He wouldn't care.
Vi You don't think so?
Harvey He's only interested in his ten per cent.
Vi That's hardly fair.
Harvey I don't feel like being fair. He probably asked to speak second — leaving me to look like some glorified warm-up man.
Vi Don't look at it like that. Look at it like this — if you go first he won't be able to steal your material.
Harvey He won't have to. No one remembers the man who speaks first.

Vi looks out of the window again

Vi I still can't believe it. He always mocked her.
Harvey Who did?
Vi Dave. He called her the stick insect.
Harvey That didn't mean anything. That was his way. Remember what he'd say to you?
Vi (*coldly*) No.
Harvey (*grinning*) You do. He'd say, "Pull up a couple of chairs and sit down, Vi".
Vi Yes. (*Drily*) How we all laughed.
Harvey That was Dave — anything for a laugh.
Vi Do you think it was a laugh — to involve you in the affair — making you lie to Laura?
Harvey I was his friend. He had no one else he could trust. He knew I'd do anything for him just as he would do anything for me. You wouldn't understand.
Vi You didn't like it when he ran into your car.
Harvey It was a new car. He paid for the repairs.
Vi You never felt the same about it though, did you?
Harvey (*smiling*) It's too late, Vi. It's too late to try and turn me against him now. The poor bugger's dead.

Vi Yes, he's dead. And be honest, aren't you a little relieved it wasn't you?

Harvey No.

Vi But you wouldn't swap places. And when you leave that churchyard today there'll be an extra spring in your stride because you're alive and he's dead.

Harvey No!

Vi Are you sure? If someone has to be in that box — wouldn't you sooner it was him than you?

Harvey No.

Vi looks at Harvey doubtfully

I'd sooner it was Kevin Prewitt.

Vi Harvey, that's an awful thing to say.

Harvey Is it? Do you know when he heard the news — he burst into tears.

Vi Well, that shows feeling.

Harvey He was in the hotel dining-room when the call came through. He burst into tears — then sat down and ate a full English breakfast.

Vi He had to eat.

Harvey Later that morning he had his blood pressure checked.

Vi Because of the breakfast?

Harvey Because of Dave.

Vi Is he another one who's insincere?

Harvey His only concern is for himself. Look at him schmoozing around the celebrities — now he has a vacancy on his list.

Vi He's wearing dark glasses.

Harvey That's to persuade us he's been weeping. He only succeeds in looking like one of the Blues Brothers.

Vi He's seen us. He's coming. You won't say anything about Jane?

Harvey Of course I won't. I'm not maligning Dave.

Vi And you will be nice to him?

Harvey (*darkly*) Don't let's get carried away.

Kevin Prewitt enters from the garden. He is a slim, pale man in his 30s. He is dressed in black with dark glasses. He has a handkerchief in his hand. He stumbles a little blindly against the furniture

Kevin (*peering*) Vi? (*He crosses to Vi and embraces her in a gesture of shared grief*)

Harvey watches him sourly. Kevin embraces Harvey in turn. Harvey looks uncomfortable

Vi Are you all right, Kevin?
Kevin They say I look dreadful.
Harvey You do.
Kevin I still can't accept it.
Harvey Dave's had to.
Kevin Jane had to drive me down.
Harvey Why?
Kevin My eyes were blurred. I couldn't focus. I couldn't have driven a car. (*He removes his glasses and dabs his eyes*)

Harvey examines Kevin's eyes suspiciously. Kevin replaces his glasses

Harvey Well, you always were more sensitive than the rest of us, Kevin — that's why you stutter.

Vi frowns

Kevin He was like a father to me, Vi.
Vi I know.
Kevin And so loyal. After the film everyone wanted him. Suddenly he was a mega-star. He could have gone to ICM — William Morris — anyone. But he stayed with me. Do you know what he said? "I started with you, Kev — and I'll finish with you." That meant a great deal ... (*His voice breaks*)
Vi I'm sure it did, Kevin.

Kevin looks around

Kevin Sorry, Vi — I can't see you very well ...
Harvey That's because you're wearing shades.

Kevin crosses, turns, and leans back against the coffin

Kevin To think there's no room in this great wide world for Dave Thursby. That I'll never see him again.
Harvey You can see him again if you want to.
Kevin I didn't know you were religious, Harvey.
Harvey I'm not, but you're leaning against him.
Kevin What! (*He turns and springs back from the coffin. He snatches off his glasses*) My God! Laura didn't say he was here!
Vi She probably thought it would upset you.
Kevin It has. I thought he'd be in a chapel of rest.
Harvey So did I.

Kevin moves further back from the coffin

Kevin It's open ...
Harvey Yes. Would you like to see him?
Vi Harvey, you can see Kevin's distressed.
Harvey I think Laura would appreciate it. You being such a close friend ...
Kevin The truth is, Harvey. I've never actually seen a dead body before.
Harvey Never?
Kevin Well, not in a live situation.
Harvey This isn't a live situation — it's a dead situation.
Kevin I mean, I've seen them on film but it's not the same, is it? I don't know how I'll react. When the news came through about Dave — I felt terrible — totally numb suddenly as if I'd been wrapped in warm cotton wool — not able to believe it.
**Harvey** Was that after the fried breakfast?
Vi Harvey ...
Harvey You mean you've reached your age without seeing a dead body?
Kevin Well, yes.
Harvey How did you manage that?
Vi By not looking into coffins, Harvey.
Harvey Then it's time he did.

Kevin hesitates

Kevin I'm not sure, Harve ... (*He pours himself a drink*)
Harvey I think you owe it to Dave.
Vi He doesn't owe it to Dave, Harvey.
Harvey Then he owes it to himself. Going round wrapped in warm cotton wool — not able to believe it. He'll believe it when he sees it.
Vi Harvey, you can see how pale he's become.
Harvey You're not going to throw up, are you, Kev?
Kevin No.
Harvey I mean if you feel squeamish ...
Kevin I'm not squeamish. (*He takes a deep drink, puts down the glass and looks into the coffin*) Oh. He looks so ——
Vi Lifelike?
Kevin No.
Harvey Pissed off?
Vi Harvey.
Kevin No, sort of amused ...

Harvey Amused? (*He takes a second look in the coffin*)
Kevin As if he's about to come out with a one-liner.
Vi Are you sure?
Kevin Yes, as if he's about to speak.
Harvey If he does you'll shit yourself.
Vi Harvey!
Kevin It's strange to think we'll never hear him tell another joke.

Harvey moves close to Kevin's ear and talks out of the corner of his mouth in an impersonation of Dave

Harvey Hey, Kev. Have you heard this one?

Kevin starts back

Vi That's not funny, Harvey.
Kevin That's all right, Vi. Harvey can't help it — he writes comedy. It startled me because I was half expecting Dave to sit up.
Harvey (*darkly*) That comes later.
Kevin What?
Harvey He will when they throw the switch. At the crematorium. (*He watches the effect of his words on Kevin*) They sit up ... swell up ... and blow up. It's the heat.
Kevin For God's sake, Harvey. I don't want to think about it. I have to speak this afternoon. I don't know if I can get through as it is.
Harvey I was told you were going second.
Kevin Yes.
Harvey Why?
Kevin It was Laura's idea. But I think it would be better if you went second.
Harvey (*pleased*) You do?
Kevin Yes.
Harvey (*frowning*) Why?
Kevin You were his oldest friend. You knew him before any of us. I think it would be more fitting.
Harvey Well, if you don't mind.
Kevin No.
Harvey Will you tell Laura?
Kevin Of course. It's not as if I've got much to say. I'm not a writer. I've just made a few notes, that's all. (*He takes out some notes*)
Vi I'm sure you'll be fine, Kevin.
Harvey Of course you will.
Kevin I'll start by mentioning his philosophy — "love and laughter".

Harvey's smile begins to fade

Then his old adage: "Make them laugh — make them cry — but above all make them wait." I'll say: "He's made us laugh — now he's made us cry — and now we have to wait in the hope we'll see Dave again."
Vi That's beautiful, Kevin.

Harvey is scowling

Kevin Then I remembered something else he always said and I'll finish with that. "We're only the laughter makers — we're not important in the scheme of things. We can't cure the ills of the world — all we can do is help to bind the wounds ..."
Vi That's a wonderful finish, Kevin.

Harvey's scowl becomes even darker

Kevin Then I'll leave it to Harve.

Without saying a word Harvey takes another sheet from his notes, crumples it and throws it in the bin

I'm not treading on your toes, am I, Harve?
Harvey Not at all.
Kevin I know it's a little solemn but Harve will win them back with some of his broad comedy.
Harvey (*frowning*) Broad?
Kevin That's what Laura needs. She's taken it so badly. She needs to laugh again.
Harvey She doesn't seem to have any trouble laughing.
Kevin I think she's on something.
Vi That's what I thought.
Kevin But deep down ...
Vi Yes.
Harvey Deep down — what?
Kevin Harvey, you may have known Dave — but I know Laura. And she's very upset.
Harvey The only thing that would upset Laura is a ring on that coffee table. She'll be married by next year.
Kevin That's where you're wrong, Harvey. You don't know her. You've never tried to get to know her. That's always saddened me. She can't talk to you. She needs someone to confide in. Fortunately, there's always me.

Harvey She confides in you?

Kevin Yes, in fact, she told me something this afternoon that's quite incredible — and very confidential. About Dave. I wish I could tell you but I can't. Laura won't confide in you.

Harvey Dave didn't have any secrets from me. I could tell you something — very confidential.

Vi Harvey ...

Harvey But I won't.

Kevin studies him for a moment

Kevin Good. Because this is a very tricky time for all of us. We don't want anything coming out of the woodwork.

Harvey What do you mean?

Kevin I mean the press. When a famous man dies he has his detractors. Stories begin to circulate. And do you know why? Because a dead man can't sue. It's something we have to remember. Dave still has a considerable shelf life.

Harvey Shelf life!

Kevin They want to repeat his last four series as a tribute.

Harvey I didn't know that.

Kevin They rang me today. And do you know why they want to repeat them? Why the whole nation mourns? Because of Dave's likeability factor. Every mother wanted him for a son — every wife for a husband — every child for a father. He was family viewing, Harve. We have to protect that.

Vi Do we have to protect it?

Kevin Yes. I've had to protect it already.

Harvey Why?

Kevin They say death cancels all debts. But not according to the Inland Revenue. The day after Dave died the tax inspectors were round to dig up the drains. Asking awkward questions. Apparently Dave was a little economical with the truth where his tax affairs were concerned. And there were some charitable donations that are proving difficult to trace ...

Harvey You mean he was fiddling? I don't believe it. Not Dave.

Kevin (*frowning*) That's the sort of terminology we should try to avoid, Harvey. We need to protect his image. We'll need Dave for years to come — you above all people.

Harvey What makes you say that?

Kevin Let's face it. You'll never find another Dave, will you?

Harvey And Dave could never find another me. He was living in a shoe box in Earls Court when I met him. They were my lines — he always said ——

Kevin Harve, it was the drunken pianist sketch that made him famous — he's never done anything better. And you didn't write that. He was doing it before he met you.

Harvey I wrote everything else. The series — the films — and I could do it again.

Kevin Could you? Perhaps you're right. But you know what they said?

Harvey No, what did they say?

Kevin That Dave could have read the telephone directory and still been funny ...

Kevin exits into the garden

Harvey and Vi look at each other in silence

Vi You asked for that.

Harvey Did I?

Vi You would keep needling him.

Harvey I like needling him. I didn't needle him enough.

Vi You mentioned his stutter.

Harvey He didn't stutter.

Vi No, he only did that with Dave.

Harvey He'd have stuttered if I'd told him about Jane ...

Vi (*shocked*) You wouldn't.

Harvey No. We have to remember the likeability factor. Did you hear what he said? Dave still has a considerable shelf life. My God!

Vi Why are you so sure it's Jane?

Harvey There were signs. She always coloured up when he spoke to her.

Vi I don't call that a sign. He always made Jane blush — just as he made Kevin stammer. He had that effect — it was his presence.

Harvey (*thoughtfully*) You don't think Dave said that, do you?

Vi What?

Harvey That he could be funny reading the telephone directory?

Vi No. He always respected what you did. He valued the words.

Harvey I may have written the words, Vi, but he provided the punctuation. His whole body could form a question mark, the twist of his head was an exclamation, his eyes blazed italics, and that open-mouthed stare was a line of dots going into infinity. He was unique.

Vi So were your words.

Harvey (*frowning*) He sometimes called them rhubarb.

Vi Did he?

Harvey When we were in rehearsal. He'd say: "I cross here, rhubarb, rhubarb. I open the door, rhubarb, rhubarb. You come in, rhubarb, rhubarb, rhubarb."

Vi That doesn't mean anything.

Harvey It does when you're writing the rhubarb, Vi.

Vi Kevin probably said that about the telephone directory to irritate you.

Harvey Yes. Notice he's going to speak first ...

Vi You wanted him to speak first.

Harvey He wanted to speak first so that he could steal my material. Quoting Dave like that. I was going to quote Dave.

Vi Well, go first.

Harvey I can't — not now.

Vi Still, it was good news about the repeats.

Harvey This is not the time to rejoice about the repeats.

Vi But it does mean you don't have to take the first offer that comes along. Perhaps you could start on the play.

Harvey The play?

Vi You said you would if you ever had the chance. Now you have the chance.

Harvey Yes, well, I'll have to think about that. (*Pause. He considers*) I wonder what it was?

Vi What?

Harvey The something Laura told him that he couldn't tell us?

Vi I don't know.

Harvey Probably nothing. Just trying to make himself important. (*He returns to the drinks tray*)

Vi Should we go into the garden?

Harvey I'll just freshen my drink ...

Jane Prewitt enters from the garden looking flustered. She is a woman of about 30, thin and gawky

Vi Something the matter, Jane?

Jane I think we may have a gatecrasher.

Vi What?

Jane We stressed family and friends — not members of the public. They are around the front gate — we can't do anything about that but she's come into the garden.

Harvey looks out

Harvey You think she's a punter?

Jane Well, she's all in black but I don't think she's one of us.

Vi Are you sure?

Jane Well, no one seems to know her — and she's not quite ...

Vi What?

Jane Not quite the thing. I spoke to her. I said how nice it was to see all the ladies in black — so in keeping. And she said, "Oh, yes, I'm in mourning right down to my knickers." Then showed me them.

Harvey (*chuckling*) Did what?

Jane Pulled up her skirt and showed me her panties — fringed with black lace. The bishop almost jumped out of his gaiters. Well, he would have done if he'd been wearing gaiters. I think she was trying to shock us.

Harvey Sounds as if she succeeded.

Vi Perhaps she was someone from the media.

Jane Showing her knickers.

Harvey Could be Channel Four.

Jane Whoever she is — she's irredeemably common.

Vi What does Laura think?

Jane I don't know. I saw her looking. I think Laura thinks she's something to do with the caterers. She handed her an empty plate.

Vi Perhaps she is.

Jane No. She was eating the sandwiches not serving them. She consumed a whole plate of egg and cress and then started on the small pork pies — and she was smoking at the same time and drinking.

Harvey Ah, what you have there, Jane, is a journalist. Kevin says we should stay away from them.

Jane I just hope she's not going to spoil things. Laura's arranged everything so beautifully. Did you see the hearse?

Harvey Yes.

Jane Laura got it from Hammer Films. There are only two in the country.

Harvey Really? Almost worth going to have a ride in one of those.

Jane I think Dave would have appreciated it.

Harvey You do?

Jane It's his sort of thing.

Harvey A glass hearse is not his sort of thing. A brewery lorry would have been his sort of thing.

Jane That's not very nice, Harvey. Don't speak ill of the dead.

Harvey I'm not.

Jane The public expect it. They expect Dave to go out with a bang.

Harvey You're not letting off fireworks as well, are you?

Jane (*sighing*) Harvey.

Vi I wouldn't take any notice of Harvey. He thinks he has the monopoly on grief at the moment. I think you've organized things very well.

Jane Thank you. Oh, Vi, we're walking up to the church — behind the hearse — in solemn cortège — so I hope you're wearing sensible shoes.

Vi (*staring*) Walking?

Jane It's only a few hundred yards.

Vi But it's uphill.

Harvey (*grinning*) Vi, if the horses can manage it, surely you can? I know they're in better shape but they are pulling the hearse.

Vi frowns at Harvey

Jane Aren't those horses magnificent? Black as night — and the coachmen — all in black too. Oh, and the dog ...

Harvey Is he in black too?

Jane Laura said would you walk him to the church.

Harvey (*staring*) Me?

Jane Yes.

Harvey Why does the dog have to go?

Jane They were very close.

Harvey Were they?

Jane Bruno's been very upset ever since it happened — scratching himself raw and eating next to nothing. Laura thought it would be nice — a last walk with his master — and it might calm him down. If you don't mind.

Vi (*amused*) Harvey doesn't mind. He's fond of animals.

Harvey Fond of animals! I've got a goldfish. Why pick on me? I've got to give an address. Why me? Why not Kevin?

Jane Dogs bring on his asthma. Besides, Laura noticed that Bruno took to you straight away.

Harvey He didn't take to me. He mounted my leg — and he wouldn't let go. I was dragging him around the house for ten minutes.

Jane He was being affectionate.

Harvey He wasn't being affectionate. He needs castrating.

Jane Laura thought it would be a wonderful photo opportunity for the press.

Harvey hesitates

Harvey Would it?

Jane A picture of the faithful hound ...

Vi (*drily*) Which one?

Jane It'll be in all the papers.

Harvey What do I do with him once I get there?

Jane Tie him to the railing outside the church — but well away from the porch — he howls at organ music.

Harvey I knew it. It's going to be a disaster. He'll howl through my valediction.

Jane That won't be longer than five minutes, will it?

Harvey (*suspiciously*) Why?

Jane Everything's been timed.

Harvey How long is Kevin speaking for?

Jane The same. It's important we don't overrun. The local flying club are going to fly over the church shortly after two.

Harvey What for?

Jane To dip their wings. As a mark of respect.

Harvey But he wasn't even a member. He hated flying.

Jane They wanted to make a gesture. Everyone does. After that the coffin will be transferred to a motorized hearse and proceed to the crematorium — followed by a select few.

Vi Not on foot?

Jane No — we'll follow in our own transport. (*She glances at her watch and moves towards the french windows*) So if you've finished in here ... The undertakers would like to come in and finish off ...

Harvey Aren't you going to have a last look at him?

Jane (*uneasily*) What?

Harvey The man this is all in aid of? The person responsible for this charade?

Jane No.

Harvey No? And you were so close ...

Vi Harve, if Jane doesn't want to see him —

Harvey So it's two hymns — a five minute chat — the wing dipping — then off to the crem — then back for a ham tea. Don't you think he's worth more than that?

Jane (*coldly*) You don't have to stay in here, Harve. There are *drinks* in the other room.

Harvey takes Jane's arm

Harvey Are you sure you don't want to see him?

Jane (*pulling away*) I want to remember him as he was.

Harvey As he was? How was he? Tell us.

Jane breaks free and moves away towards the garden. She turns

Jane Harvey, this afternoon — don't make it too broad.

Harvey Broad?
Jane Not too many one-liners — it is a church service.

Jane exits

Harvey Did you hear that? Not too many one-liners? That's how humourless people refer to wit. Because they can't do it themselves they denigrate it by the term "one-liners". They didn't say that to Oscar Wilde — sorry, too many one-liners, Oscar.
Vi She didn't blush.
Harvey What?
Vi Just now.
Harvey Dave wasn't here.
Vi You could be wrong.
Harvey (*shrugging*) I could be. What do I know? I'm only the dog handler. That was another put-down. They're trying to humiliate me.
Vi No — Laura thought Bruno was fond of you.
Harvey He's fond of my leg, that's all. I can just see me walking behind the hearse — Bruno hanging on to my leg with all four paws — me trying to kick him off ... (*His voice dies away*)

Kay enters hesitantly from the garden. She is in her 50s but still retains a trim figure. Her black dress is close fitting and short. She is smoking

Vi Can we help you?
Kay I wondered if I could have a peep?
Harvey Have a peep? It's not a peep show.
Kay I realize that. I just felt I should.
Vi Did Mrs Thursby say you could?
Kay No. I haven't spoken to Mrs Thursby. It won't hurt, will it?
Vi I don't think Mrs Thursby would like you smoking in here.
Harvey He doesn't want ash spilling on him.
Kay Sorry. (*She puts out her cigarette*)
Vi This room is reserved for family and close friends.
Kay I realize that. I am family.
Harvey (*doubtfully*) Not on Dave's side.
Kay Yes.
Harvey He never mentioned any family to me. (*He studies Kay*) You don't look like a relative.
Kay By marriage, but if you feel ... (*She backs towards the garden*)
Harvey No, wait a minute. What's your name? At the moment we only know you as the woman in black, which isn't much use on a day like this. Who are you?

Kay Kay Thursby.
Harvey (*stunned*) Kay ...?
Kay Thursby. I kept my married name.
Harvey (*blankly*) You did?

Silence

Vi I think I can hear a pin drop.
Harvey (*slowly*) You mean ... you mean you were ... you mean you
were married ... you were married to ...
Vi (*smiling*) Finish your sentence, Harve.
Kay To Dave Thursby. Years ago.
Harvey Years ago?
Kay Cromer.
Harvey Cromer?
Kay Summer season.
Harvey Summer season.
Vi Well, in that case, I think you have every right to see him. (*She
motions Kay across to the coffin*)

Kay studies the body in silence

Do you think he's changed much?
Harvey (*sharply*) Of course he's changed — he's dead.
Kay I must say I've seen him in better shape — death can be very
ageing. But he hasn't changed much. It's amazing what they can do.
Harvey I don't care what they can do. He must have changed since
Cromer.
Kay But not since a few weeks ago.
Harvey You saw him a few weeks ago?
Kay Yes. We saw each other regularly.
Harvey Oh, did you? Well, I was his closest friend and I didn't know
anything about this. He couldn't have seen you on a regular basis —
not without me knowing. And then there's Laura — what about her?
Kay That wasn't a problem. Dave had one of his minions to cover for him.
Harvey Minions!
Vi Then Laura doesn't know about you?
Kay No.
Vi Not a good day for her to find out.
Kay (*shrugging*) She has to know sometime.
Harvey (*suspiciously*) Why?
Kay I expect her to keep up the payments.
Harvey So that's it. You've come for money. Now Dave's dead and
can't deny it.

Kay He couldn't deny it when he was alive.

Harvey So you say. And what's this about Cromer? He never played Cromer. I would have known. I knew every date he ever played.

Kay He wasn't known as Dave Thursby in those days. His stage name was Fred Freak.

Vi Fred Freak?

Harvey Fred Freak! My God!

Kay He wasn't very good. He was second comic. I was in the chorus. Tommy Traddles was top billing. He held the show together with his drunken pianist sketch.

Harvey If you think I'm going to listen to this ... (*He tails off*) Did you say drunken pianist sketch?

Kay Yes.

Harvey But that was Dave's.

Kay No, Dave learned it from Tommy. He watched him in the wings every night. I remember him turning to me and saying, "That's pure gold, Kay." Unfortunately Tommy played the drunk after the show too. He'd sit drinking with Dave for hours — then he'd go home along the cliff path. One night he went over. Whether he fell or jumped, no one was certain. I think Dave probably pushed him.

Harvey and Vi stare at her waiting for the laugh

Vi You're joking.

Kay Am I? I always say, think of the worst thing he could do — and then double it — and that's Dave.

Harvey You must be talking about someone else. That's not the Dave we knew.

Kay The next night he was doing the drunken pianist sketch ...

Vi But you married him.

Kay That's the sort of thing you did then. It didn't last long. When he found out I was pregnant he took what was left of our money and went.

Vi Where did he go?

Kay I heard a rumour he was working the cruise ships.

Vi Didn't you try and find him?

Kay Why? He wouldn't support me and I certainly couldn't support him — not with a child. I went to live with my sister in Australia. Came back a few years ago, switched on the TV and there he was, still doing the drunken pianist sketch.

Vi Is that when you asked him for money?

Kay He owed me. I had to raise a son and put him through college. I was entitled.

Vi And he paid?

Kay Yes — used notes in a plain envelope. Nothing you could trace.

Harvey How convenient.

Kay (*shrugging*) You know Dave.

Harvey Not from your description, I don't. And you came back into his life — on a regular basis — even though he'd abandoned you?

Kay I wasn't the first person he'd abandoned. He abandoned his own mother.

Vi (*shocked*) He abandoned his mother?

Kay After his father died she was destitute. He didn't care. Even though he was partly to blame for his father's death.

Vi How was he to blame?

Harvey Did he push him over a cliff?

Kay No. He set him on fire.

Vi He set fire to his own father?

Kay That's what he told me. Well, he set fire to his bed which was almost the same thing, isn't it?

Vi Why?

Kay He said it was the only way he could get him out of it but I think he was joking. His father was a drunk. One day, when Dave was sixteen, the old man punished him for stealing.

Harvey Stealing!

Kay While his father was sleeping it off Dave packed a little suitcase, put a match to his father's mattress and went into show business. His father had a heart attack a few years later — I don't think he ever got over waking up in a bed of flames — then his mother came asking for money. He told her to get lost.

Vi How could he do that?

Kay He blamed his mother for everything. For marrying his father — his lack of background — his lack of education — even his lack of clean underwear. She got all the blame — until he met me. Then he started blaming me.

Vi What for?

Kay The same things — except possibly the underwear. He said I was holding him back. He was always ruthlessly ambitious. He wouldn't let anyone stand in his way.

Harvey (*angrily*) I don't believe any of this! Not about his drunken father — his grey-haired old mother — or his abandoned wife and child. You try selling that story to the newspaper and we'll sue.

Vi We can't, Harve. It's nothing to do with us.

Harvey It has something to do with me.

Vi Dave's dead. She can say what she likes. It doesn't have to be true.

Harvey It isn't true.

Vi But it's damaging. You're forgetting something — Dave's likeability factor ...

Harvey (*coldly*) I hadn't thought about that, Vi.
Vi I'm sure Kay has. I think we'd better get Kevin.
Harvey Yes, get Kevin.

Vi exits into the garden

He has friends in the police. He'll know how to deal with this. Tell him.
Tell him we're being blackmailed. He'll know what to do. (*Glaring
furiously at Kay*) Everyone loved Dave. Even his dog is pining for him
and clinging to people in grief. Dave was gentle — he wouldn't have
set fire to a man's mattress.
Kay Well, perhaps he changed over the years.
Harvey He didn't change. I'm not saying you didn't know him. He
may even have married you. The rest is bile, bitterness and rancour.
Women! You won't even let him rest in peace. He was a decent man
— and you're not going to feed him to the press.
Kay I don't intend to.
Harvey Good, because Kevin's an agent. He's used to the seamy side
of life. He'll know how to deal with you. Or perhaps you've spoken
to him already?
Kay No — not after what Dave said.

Harvey stops in mid-flight

Harvey What did Dave say?
Kay He didn't trust him.
Harvey He didn't?
Kay No.
Harvey (*with a slow smile*) Didn't trust him?
Kay That's what he said. Never really liked him either.
Harvey Never liked him. I thought not. Kevin always thought he had
this special relationship but I never bought it. Dave had this way of
looking at him ...
Kay He thought he was a lousy agent.
Harvey He is a lousy agent. He couldn't find work in a job centre. I
don't know why Dave stayed.
Kay He was going to leave him.
Harvey (*beaming*) Was he?
Kay He was going to William Morris. He wanted someone worldwide.
He said Kevin was small time.
Harvey He is — you couldn't find anyone smaller. (*Laughing*) So that's
what Dave meant. "I started with you, Kevin and I'll finish with you."
He was going to finish with him all right!

Kay But then he died.

Harvey returns to earth

Harvey Yes.

*Kevin enters with Vi. He closes the french windows with great care.
He turns*

Kevin, this is —
Kevin I know. Let me recap on what I've been told. You say you're Kay
Thursby — that you were married to Dave — and you had his child —
and you've come for money.
Kay Yes.
Kevin Do you have any proof?
Kay Not with me.
Kevin Not with you. So there's not a shred of evidence — just your
word.
Kay Yes.
Kevin And you chose today, of all days, to come forward with this
story. When it could cause the most damage.
Kay I don't want to cause any trouble. I just want the arrangement to
continue.
Kevin Can you prove there was an arrangement?
Kay Not at the moment.
Kevin Not at the moment. And you think we're going to pay you money
— or rather Mrs Thursby's going to pay you money — simply because
you ask for it? There is a law in this country to protect people from
extortion and blackmail.
Harvey Listen to what he's saying.
Kevin Please, Harvey. On the other hand we would like the funeral to
take place with the minimum of fuss.
Harvey What are you talking about? It's had the maximum of fuss
already — it can't take any more.
Kevin Let me deal with this, Harvey. After all, there's Laura to consider.
We could come to some small arrangement — to tide you over —
Harvey Small arrangement!
Kevin I'm mending fences here, Harvey. Some small arrangement in
return for which we'd expect you to exercise discretion.
Harvey Discretion! She doesn't know the meaning of the word.
According to her — Dave may have pushed an old comedian off a cliff
— thrown his grey-haired mother on to the streets — and attempted to
cremate his father before his time!

Kevin Harvey, if you don't mind — we're trying to achieve a little damage limitation ...

Jane enters from the garden. She sees Kay and starts

Jane So there you are. I've been looking for you. What are you doing here?

Vi She wanted to see Dave.

Jane Wanted to see Dave! He's not a public spectacle.

Kevin The point is — she claims to have been married to Dave.

Jane What!

Kevin She also claims he owes her money — sort of maintenance.

Jane I see. Well, that's easy to say, isn't it? Now he's not here to deny it.

Kevin I have made that point.

Jane As if Dave would have married a woman like that.

Kay What?

Jane Dave would never have married a woman like that. He always had taste.

Kay If you don't mind I don't wish to be referred to as "a woman like that".

Jane Then I suggest you leave. Why don't you throw her out, Kevin?

Kevin Jane, don't let's be hasty. I'm attempting a little damage limitation here ...

Kay Oh. So you're Jane.

Jane Yes.

Kay He talked about you.

Jane Did he?

Kay You and the fun and games in the stationery cupboard.

Silence

Kevin What was that? What does she mean?

Jane I don't know what she means.

Kay Then you don't know Dave. You don't think he'd kiss and not tell, do you? He told me all about it. All about those Thursday nights. When you stayed late at the office for the payroll run — those moments of bliss in the stationery cupboard.

Kevin and Jane exchange glances. Harvey hands Kevin his drink with a false smile of sympathy

Kevin Did Dave come to the office on Thursdays?

Jane Well, yes but —
Kevin You never told me.
Jane It wasn't important.
Kevin Important enough to keep it quiet. (*He grimaces*) The stationery cupboard.
Jane It's not a cupboard — it's a stationery store.
Kevin It's a cupboard! You couldn't swing a cat round in it!
Kay (*drily*) Dave did, apparently.
Kevin So that's why you stayed late. How deceitful. How Dave must have hated it.
Jane (*staring*) Hated what?
Kevin The deception. You planned it didn't you? You always meant to come between us. You were so jealous.
Jane Jealous. I didn't come between you. He loathed you. He was leaving. He was going to William Morris. He would have left years ago if it hadn't been for me.
Kevin What?
Jane Ask Harvey. He was in on it. He covered for him. He was to tell Laura Dave was working late. Ask him.

Kevin turns to Harvey

Kevin Is this true, Harvey?

Harvey backs away looking nervously at the drink

Harvey I didn't know it was Jane. He asked me to cover for him, that was all. He didn't confide in me. (*Feigning great surprise*) So it was Jane!
Kevin Loathed me? He must have been laughing at me all the time. And all the time I thought we were friends. I said he seemed to be smiling ... (*He crosses and looks into coffin. He begins to stutter*) He was laughing at me — even in death. Look at him. (*Sobbing*) The smu-smu-smu-smug ba-ba-ba-bastard. (*He raises the glass and dashes the contents into the coffin*)

There is a general gasp of shock and horror

Jane sobs and dashes out into the garden

Kevin staggers back and stares blankly at his empty glass

What have I done?

Harvey (*angrily*) I'll tell you what you've done. You've desecrated Dave. (*He snatches the glass from Kevin*)

Kevin throws himself into a chair and buries his head in his hands

Vi You didn't mean it, Kevin. You were overcome.

Harvey pats Kevin on the shoulder, complacently sympathetic

Harvey It makes you wonder. Do we really know anyone, Kev?
Kevin (*muffled*) I certainly didn't know him.
Harvey Pull yourself together, Kevin. You have an address to give.
Kevin I can't — the words would choke me.
Harvey You can't. No, I can see that. (*He begins taking the crumpled notes from the bin and straightens them*)

Vi dabs discreetly in the coffin with a hanky

Laura enters. She regards the scene curiously

Laura What's the matter, Kevin?
Vi Overcome with grief, I'm afraid.
Laura Jane's the same. She just dashed by me in tears.
Harvey It's been an emotional day for him. He won't be able to give his address.
Laura But we've got a five minute slot. Who's going to fill it?
Harvey Well, I don't mind ...
Kay I'll do it.

Laura stares at Kay

Laura I'm sorry — have we met?
Vi (*quickly*) This is Kay — from Cromer.
Laura Cromer?
Vi She did a summer season with Dave years ago — never forgot him.
Laura All those years ago — and you haven't forgotten him. Isn't that wonderful? And you've come all this way. People have been so thoughtful. But then David was someone you couldn't forget.
Kay I certainly couldn't.
Harvey I don't mind speaking for longer ...
Laura No, this is what we need. Someone to talk about the old days. Just say whatever comes into your head, Kay. You speak after: "Abide with me — fast falls the eventide." (*She turns back to Harvey*) You

follow the reading, Harvey. Corinthians. "Though I speak with the tongues of men and of angels and have not love I am become as sounding brass or tinkling symbols."

Harvey Corinthians. Perhaps Revelations would have been better.

Laura Do you think so? There will be two secular pieces. We open with his theme song "Getting to Know You" — *The King and I*. And then for the Committal we have "Somewhere Over the Rainbow" sung by Judy Garland. I know she's a gay icon but I don't think people will draw any conclusion from that.

Vi (*drily*) Not when Kay's finished remembering Cromer.

Laura Now we must hurry — the undertakers are here ... (*She looks into the coffin. She stares. She looks upward thoughtfully, then back to the body*) I know it's faintly ridiculous but it's as if David's been shedding a tear.

Harvey (*drily*) More likely to be perspiration.

Vi (*quickly*) Yes, I think it's time we ...

Laura You're right, one has to let go. (*She takes Kay's arm*) Come with me, Kay, you'll be my special guest.

All except Kevin move out into the garden

Kevin remains slumped

Harvey returns. He is obviously enjoying himself

Harvey Come on, Kevin. The body snatchers will be here any minute. We don't want them taking you as well.

Kevin I still can't believe it, Harve.

Harvey Do we really know anyone? You thought you knew two people — today you found out you didn't.

Kevin So you do believe it?

Harvey Afraid so ...

Kevin You think he really was going to William Morris?

Harvey stares

CURTAIN

ACT II

The same. Three weeks later. Afternoon

*The room is unchanged except that the sideboard has been moved back
to where the coffin stood. On the sideboard is a brass urn with handles,
under a spotlight. The curtains are wide open. The day is overcast*

*Sound of conversation off. Harvey and Vi enter the room. Vi's outfit is
still fairly subdued. Harvey is wearing a light suit and tie. He looks back
suspiciously*

Harvey Why did she wave us through here?
Vi Can't you guess? (*She indicates the urn*)

Harvey turns and sees the urn for the first time. He starts

Harvey (*reading the urn*) Wentworth. Pro-am ... Fourball!
Vi Only thing he ever won. Laura thought it would be a nice touch.
Harvey Couldn't she have left it at the crematorium?
Vi She couldn't just leave it there, Harve.
Harvey Of course she could — it's not a takeaway. She could have
had them sprinkled round the rose bushes. Now he has to stand on the
sideboard for the next fifty years.
Vi He's not going to stand on the sideboard. That's why we're here.
Harvey What?
Vi For the disposal of the ashes.
Harvey (*sarcastically*) Damn! And I thought they were reading the
will.
Vi He didn't leave a will.
Harvey I wouldn't have come if I'd known.
Vi That's why I didn't tell you. (*She regards his suit*) I just hope that
suit's going to be all right.
Harvey It'll have to be. Why do they have to drag things out like this?
First the church service — then the cremation — then the dispersal of
the ashes — and next month, a service of remembrance before we've
had time to forget him. Do me a favour. When it's my turn — leave
me by the roadside.
Vi (*smiling mockingly*) I couldn't. There's a law against fly-tipping.
Should you be talking like this in front of Dave?

Harvey regards the urn moodily

Harvey If it is Dave.
Vi What do you mean? Of course it's Dave — or what's left of him.
Harvey Not necessarily. They don't do one at a time down there.
Wouldn't be worth putting the oven on. They usually wait until
there's half a dozen — it's like a mixed grill. And if they're a bit
casual scooping out the ashes — you could have a couple of old-aged
pensioners in there with him.
Vi Harve!
Harvey There could be more than a fourball in there.
Vi Well, it's only symbolic, isn't it? Ashes to ashes, dust to dust, if the
Lord doesn't get you, the devil must. *(She smiles)* Well, we've got a
good idea who's going to get Dave.
Harvey *(frowning)* What do you mean by that?
Vi Well, after what Kay said ...
Harvey You didn't believe all that, did you?
Vi Didn't you?
Harvey She didn't repeat it in her funeral oration, did she? All we had
was a few friendly reminiscences.
Vi I think that was out of respect for Laura.
Harvey Or a belated respect for the truth.
Vi You didn't believe anything she said?
Harvey I didn't say that. All I'm saying is I didn't hear anything that
changed my feelings for Dave. He's still my friend.
Vi He was — was your friend.
Harvey I don't condemn him. You know his weakness? Women. I tried
to explain this to Kevin.
Vi You don't think he was being deceitful?
Harvey No. He was being what they wanted him to be. That's what I
told Kevin. Those women each had a different perception of Dave.
And when people have a perception of us — we tend to become that
perception. Jane wanted him to follow her into that cupboard and
ravish her amongst the stationery. He did. Laura, of the sacred lips,
wanted him to worship her as an immaculate goddess. He did.
Vi And what about Kay?
Harvey She wanted to be bullied and trampled on. He did.
Vi I still think he was being deceitful.
Harvey Dave was not deceitful. He was fiercely loyal to his friends.
Vi Oh. And what about Kevin?
Harvey Kevin wasn't his friend. How could he have a friend like
Kevin?
Vi Do you know, it makes me wonder if Dave had any friends apart
from you.

Harvey What! You were at the funeral — the church was full.

Vi Yes, but most of them were smiling.

Harvey (*fiercely*) They were fighting back the tears. I know I was.

Vi Yes but he was very special to you, wasn't he?

Harvey What are you implying?

Vi Nothing, except that you have this possessiveness about Dave. I suppose it was because you were an only child.

Harvey What has being an only child got to do with it?

Vi They have difficulty sharing. You have difficulty sharing Dave. With Laura, with Jane, with Kay. What really annoyed you at the funeral was the discovery that Dave had a life in Cromer under the name of Fred Freak. And you didn't even know.

Harvey I didn't want to know. He didn't want me to know. He wanted to bury the past. And who can blame him. My God. Fred Freak! (*He picks up the urn*)

> "Alas poor Fred,
> He was alive.
> Now he's dead.
> There's no more to be said."

(*Putting down the urn; regarding it*) One thing that did please me ...

Vi What?

Harvey He stole the drunken pianist sketch. The one thing I didn't write ...

Vi And that makes you feel better?

Harvey Yes. He needed me, Vi.

Vi I always said so.

Harvey What's she going to do with these? (*He gestures to the ashes*)

Vi I'm not sure. Her first thought was to sprinkle them from an aeroplane.

Harvey Not the flying club again! I've told you he hated flying.

Vi She wanted them to be spread as wide and as far as his fame. Then she thought they might blow back in the pilot's face and blind him. So she changed her mind. Then she thought of the fifteenth hole at Wentworth ...

Harvey The fifteenth hole! Is she a sadist? He hated that hole. He hated that hole more than flying.

Vi She thought of spreading him on the green.

Harvey If she did, it would have been the first time he'd been on it.

Vi Then she thought of all those spiked shoes ...

Harvey Spiked shoes! Dear Lord! He wouldn't feel anything! When is she going to realize? Four weeks ago Dave was a man — then he was a husk — now he's dust. (*He holds up the urn*) There's no personality here — no feelings. The only place Dave exists is in our minds — not in here.

Vi So she's decided to sprinkle them on the bottom lawn. At least that was her last thought.

Harvey Will there be many to witness this sacred event?

Vi The local vicar — and a few more. Kevin's here.

Harvey After all that's happened?

Vi Yes. So don't mention the stationery cupboard. He's bound to be sensitive about it.

Harvey He can't be so sensitive — he's here.

Vi He still represents Dave. And with the repeats and the retrospectives. Dave's busier than when he was alive.

Harvey Good old Dave. Still looking out for us.

Vi It means you can write that play.

Harvey Yes ... (*He hesitates*) There's something else I want to write first ...

Vi What's that?

Harvey (*after a pause*) Dave's biography.

Vi (*staring*) His biography? You've never mentioned that before. When did you have that idea?

Harvey Recently.

Vi Recently. Since the funeral?

Harvey I'm not sure when I had the idea but, after all, why not? No one was closer to Dave than I was — and who knows more about him?

Vi You certainly know more about him now. That's what gave you the idea, isn't it? The thought that you could juice it up with all these revelations.

Harvey I wouldn't say that although it does give it more texture.

Vi Is that what you call it? Texture.

Harvey Yes.

Vi And what about Kevin and Jane? Are they going to be texture?

Harvey If I'm going to do it I have to tell the whole story, Vi.

Vi Why?

Harvey My integrity as a writer. I owe it to the public — to posterity.

Vi Posterity! What's posterity when it's at home? I'm talking about Kevin and Jane. Suppose you'd been in Kevin's position?

Harvey But I'm not. That's why I can remain dispassionate.

Vi They won't be dispassionate — not when the book comes out.

Harvey That's a long way off. I haven't even got an advance yet.

Vi Oh, so you're expecting one.

Harvey There'll be a great deal of interest. And I wouldn't worry about Kevin and Jane — they'll probably be divorced by then, they're hardly speaking as it is.

Vi Well if they're not divorced they certainly will be by the time you're finished. And what about Laura?

Harvey Laura thinks it's a good idea.

Vi You've already discussed it with her?

Harvey Yes.

Vi Does she know what you're going to put in it?

Harvey Well, we didn't discuss the contents.

Vi I'm sure you didn't.

Harvey How can I? Even I don't know what's going in it.

Vi Oh, yes, you do. She'll be appalled.

Harvey She may be but she's not the best judge. History is full of narrow-minded wives who destroyed great men's diaries because of misplaced prudishness and outraged modesty.

Vi Dave was not a great man.

Harvey I happen to think he was. At least he was a great human being. He can stand the truth.

Vi Are you sure? Aren't you forgetting something? The repeats? His likeability factor? Your book will certainly play hell with the old likeability factor.

Harvey That's where you're wrong. It'll only make him more human. Like Byron.

Vi Byron?

Harvey He was accused of almost everything in his time. Murder, bigamy, piracy, incest, sodomy, buggery and devil worship and yet there were thousands at his funeral and when they were asked why they mourned the bad Lord Byron do you know what they said? "He was such a great man, we've forgotten his faults."

Vi Dave was not Lord Byron. Your trouble is you're obsessed with him. You always have been. Can't you see, you're still making excuses for him and Harvey, you're still living off him — you'll be living off him years after he's dead.

Harvey (*angrily*) I've never lived off him —— (*He breaks off as Kevin enters*)

Kevin enters. He is wearing a dark suit and a tie of deep maroon. He nods at them bleakly and crosses to pour himself a sherry

Vi (*uneasily*) Kevin.

Kevin Vi.

Vi How are you?

Kevin Fine. (*He turns from the drinks tray to find himself confronted by the urn. He snubs it*)

Harvey (*grinning*) Surprised you're here, Kev — under the circumstances.

Vi frowns

Kevin Laura was expecting me. What could I say? I didn't want to come. You'll notice the tie. I think that says it all ...

Vi and Harvey stare at the perfectly acceptable tie

Harvey The tie?
Kevin Rather loud for me, wouldn't you say? Not what I'd normally wear on an occasion like this. I think it'll be observed.
Harvey (*smiling*) Now you mention it — it is rather bold.
Kevin One might almost say disrespectful ...?
Harvey Yes. You're making a statement, aren't you, Kev?
Kevin I just hope Laura doesn't remark on it — I may be forced to say something — something that could prove hurtful ...
Vi I wouldn't, Kevin.
Kevin Perhaps you're right. I have agreed to forgive and forget.
Harvey Hard though, isn't it, Kev? Is Jane here?

Kevin's jaw snaps

Kevin Oh yes. Here to say goodbye to a close friend. And I mean close. Have you seen the size of that stationery cupboard?
Harvey We weren't going to mention that, Kev. (*Pause*) That small?
Vi Look, Kevin, it must have been a terrible shock, I know, but it's all over — he's dead — and you're making Jane miserable. At least try to forget — forget Dave.
Kevin How can I? I'm working harder for him now than when he was alive.
Vi But he's dead.
Kevin He may be dead but there's always his residuals.
Vi I thought they were in the urn.
Kevin Oh, I know he never appreciated the work I did. I know he despised me. But what did I ever do to him — except make him rich?
Vi I thought he made you rich.
Kevin I shall continue to represent him but I shall never forgive him. Do you know he never bought her a present — never took her out — never wined and dined her — no flowers — not even a box of chocolates — just straight into that damned cupboard.

Harvey pats Kevin unctuously on the shoulder

Harvey Do we ever really know anyone, Kev?
Vi Don't blame Jane. She must have been terribly unhappy.

Kevin Are you suggesting that I made her unhappy?

Vi (*hastily*) No. I meant Dave must have made her unhappy.

Harvey Oh, I don't know. She didn't have to go into that cupboard. It couldn't have been comfortable. But she went. What prompted her? No chocolates — no wining and dining. Into the cupboard. Why? Because it was Dave. She must have felt that it was worth the sacrifice. That what happened in there was a defining moment in her life — the ultimate experience ... (*His voice dies away*)

Kevin is glaring angrily at Harvey. Harvey becomes aware of it

(*Uneasily*) Of course, that's just my perception.

Vi So we're back to perception again, are we? Well, you're not a woman. Ask Jane — ask that woman from Cromer — ask them about their perceptions.

Harvey I'd like to ask that woman from Cromer a great deal. I'm sure there's a lot she didn't tell us.

Kevin Well, now's your chance. She's here.

Harvey What! I thought we'd seen the last of her.

Kevin You don't see the last of women like that.

Vi What is she doing here?

Kevin Laura asked her to come — for the spreading of the ashes. She thought it would be nice.

Harvey Has she told Laura anything?

Kevin Not yet. It's like waiting for a bomb to go off. I couldn't take any more. That's why I came in here.

Vi Perhaps she won't say anything.

Kevin Of course she will. That's what she's here for. To put the bite on Laura.

Vi She didn't say anything at the funeral.

Kevin She was in church, wasn't she? Probably had a sobering effect but it won't last. She'll say something.

Harvey Perhaps I should have a word with her — try and calm her down.

Vi Sure you're not looking for more material?

Kevin Material?

Vi Harvey's going to write a book about Dave.

Kevin (*frowning*) A book? Do you mean a biography?

Harvey I was thinking about it ... When the dust has settled.

Kevin When the dust has settled? Well, as a particle of that dust will I be mentioned?

Harvey You were his agent, Kev. And we know he had strong feelings about you. It's all part of the picture.

Kevin And will Jane be part of the picture?

Harvey I haven't really decided what form the book will take. How much light relief — and comic incident — I should include.
Kevin Comic incident? You think of it as a comic incident?
Harvey Well, the stationery cupboard, Kev, it does have a farcical element. My bet is that in years to come you might well look back on this episode and laugh ...

Kevin is grim-faced. Harvey regards him for a moment

Well, obviously not at the moment ... But who knows?

Jane enters from the hall and crosses to get a drink

Jane and Kevin ignore each other. Jane speaks to no one in particular

Jane That woman's here. I don't know what she's going to say but I hope she doesn't say it in front of the vicar.
Kevin I'd better go through and keep an eye on things.
Jane (*bitterly*) Yes, why don't you do a little damage limitation — mend a few fences? That's what you're good at.

Kevin pauses by the door

Kevin There's not much point in mending fences. You're coming out in paperback next year.

Kevin exits

Jane (*staring*) What did he mean?
Harvey I've no idea.
Jane (*after a pause*) I suppose you think I'm terrible.
Vi No, of course we don't.
Harvey These things happen, Jane. And who are we to judge? Do we really know anyone? Take Dave. All we ever saw was the tip of the iceberg.
Jane No — not the tip of the iceberg. At least that's a warning. Dave was more like a coral island — on the surface all warm sands and Hawaiian guitars but underneath a mass of coral that could rip the heart out of you.

Silence

Harvey (*impressed*) Did you hear that? I've never heard you work a metaphor like that before. You've changed. That's Dave. He's enriched you, Jane.

Vi She doesn't look enriched.

Jane I don't feel enriched.

Harvey But you are. You have life, colour, vitality. You never had that before. To tell the truth I always found you a little drab.

Vi Harvey.

Harvey But Dave saw something in you that we missed. He was like that. He made you into a whole woman. Let me ask you this — do you really regret one moment of your time with Dave?

Jane Yes.

Harvey Even in the stationery cupboard?

Jane It was a store room! And I didn't feel enriched. He made me feel clumsy and inadequate.

Harvey Then why did he follow you in there? Was it a sudden impulse? Did you climb on a stool? Did he catch a sudden glimpse of your legs?

Jane My legs! You know how he referred to my legs — two pipe cleaners out for a walk.

Harvey That was Dave's way. He was impish, irreverent. He didn't mean it. What did he say to Vi? Pull up a couple of chairs and sit down, Vi.

Vi Yes, we've all heard that, Harvey.

Harvey I think you were special to him, Jane. And deep down, in his own way, he may have loved you.

Jane Loved me! He never said one nice thing to me.

Harvey He was laying siege, Jane. And when you besiege a city the first thing you do is undermine the confidence of the defenders. No, I think he loved you, in his own strange way. And I'll make a little bet with myself that deep down you loved him.

Jane I hated him.

Harvey What?

Vi Then why, Jane?

Jane (*tearfully*) I don't know why. All I know is that when he first put his arms around me I felt a great sense of relief — that I wasn't such a freak after all.

Vi puts her arms around Jane

Vi You're not a freak, Jane.

Jane That's how he made me feel — until then.

Laura and Kay enter from the hall. Laura is still dressed in fashionable black but without the trimmings. Kay is more casually dressed

*Laura leads Kay across to the drinks tray and begins to pour her a drink.
She glances at Jane being comforted by Vi*

Laura Poor Jane. Still missing David. I never thought she'd take it so
hard. Just the same at the funeral — totally broken up. It's amazing
how it's the strong, self-possessed ones who are the first to go and feel
it the most. I suppose it's a compliment to David that he still arouses
such strong feelings. Kate has come all the way from Cromer simply
to pay her respects.

Kay Kay.

Laura What?

Kay My name's Kay.

Laura Kay, of course.

Kay And I don't come from Cromer.

Laura What a pity. Such a nice place ... (*She crosses and admires the
urn. She turns to the room*) Do you know I had the strangest dream
about David last night. I dreamt I was holding the urn in my arms and
it slowly became really hot — and then a green flame flared out of it
and became a huge cloud — all green — and then it took shape — and
it was David. Still all green but definitely David — only twenty foot
high.

Silence

Vi You mean like a genie from a bottle?

Laura That's it — like a genie from a bottle.

Jane gives a faintly hysterical laugh

Vi (*hastily*) Did he say anything?

Laura Yes but since he was twenty feet up it was difficult to catch it.
But he sounded regretful ...

Vi I'm sure he had nothing to regret.

Laura Oh, yes, he had. There's something I should tell you — something
you don't know — about David.

They wait with bated breath.

Something I've been keeping to myself. He missed his knighthood.
Her Majesty had seen fit to honour him.

Harvey (*staring*) Are you sure? He never said anything to me.

Laura (*coldly*) He didn't tell you everything, Harvey. He was to have
appeared in the New Year's honours list.

Kay (*surprised*) What for?

Laura What for! Services to charity and his work in the field of entertainment. An honour well deserved.

Harvey You mean in a few months he'd have been Sir David Thursby?

Laura In just a few months. His death couldn't have come at a worse time.

Harvey (*upset*) He never said anything to me.

Vi That means you'd have been Lady Thursby.

Laura Oh, that didn't matter to me. I think titles are rather quaint but I wanted it for David. He'd worked so hard for it.

Vi Won't he still get it?

Harvey Of course he won't. It's not like the VC. You don't get it posthumously.

Laura He was so excited. He drove straight round to Downing Street to deliver his acceptance. He rehearsed his entry into the throne room — the bending of the knee — the walking out backwards. I played Her Majesty. He would have been perfect. (*She gestures at the urn*) And this had to happen, it couldn't have come at a worse time — on the verge of his greatest triumph.

Kay crosses and regards the urn

Kay (*chuckling*) And now he's in there. Don't tell me God hasn't got a sense of humour.

Laura What was that?

Harvey (*quickly*) I think Kay was commenting on the irony of fate.

Kevin enters

Kevin The vicar says he's ready when you are, Laura.

Laura Good. I've decided to sprinkle the ashes on the bottom lawn — near the summer house. He'd sit there watching the sunset — sipping his vodka ... smoking ... unfiltered ... and inhaling, I'm afraid. Well, now for the solemnities. I just wish your suit was a little more appropriate, Harvey. Perhaps you could merge into the background — if that's possible.

Kevin (*significantly*) What about my tie, Laura?

Laura Your tie?

Kevin I suppose you find that inappropriate?

Laura No.

Kevin Oh.

Laura moves to the french windows and then turns back to the desk. She picks up a pen

Laura Oh, Kate, the local paper wanted a list of mourners — yours seems to be the only one missing — and since you came all the way from Cromer ... could I add your name?
Kay Certainly. Kay Thursby.

Laura is about to write down the name. She stops and looks up curiously

Laura Thursby?
Kay Yes.
Laura Are you a relative?
Kay Yes.
Laura (*after a pause*) Close?
Kay Yes.
Laura (*slowly*) How close?
Kay Very close. I married Dave at Cromer registry office in nineteen seventy-nine.

Laura sits abruptly. Kay takes a paper and hands it to Laura. Laura studies the paper for a moment

Laura Why haven't you come forward before?
Kay There was no need.
Laura How do I know this is genuine?
Kay We had a son. (*She hands Laura a photograph*) You must agree there's a likeness.
Laura I don't see any likeness. (*Pause*) You've come for money, I suppose.
Kay I'm prepared to be reasonable.
Laura But I'm not. I don't know what happened in Cromer in those distant days when Adam was a boy but I can imagine. David was young and impressionable and you were a member of the chorus — probably not the only one — and if he did marry you, which I doubt, he married the pair of legs that kicked the highest.
Kevin Laura, this isn't the time for a scene — we can compromise here.
Laura That's what she's depending on, Kevin — that I'll pay her off to avoid a scandal.
Kay I don't want you to pay me off.

Laura No — I'd have to keep paying. And what happens when the rest of the chorus turns up? I'll never stop paying. No, I'm sorry, if you need money I suggest you work for it. Go back to the chorus and kick those tired old legs in the air because that's the only way you're going to get it.

Kevin Laura, this isn't a good idea.

Laura Isn't it? (*She tears up the photograph*) David was infertile. It was a great disappointment to him. He couldn't have children.

Kay He could in nineteen seventy-nine. You're forgetting — he was fresh off the assembly line then. You may have had his wealth — I had his health.

Laura And that's what you've come for, isn't it — his wealth.

Kay No — but I still have a son to look out for.

Laura Prove it. (*She crosses and picks up the urn holding it close*) You won't get much evidence out of this. And this is all that's left.

Kay I don't have to prove it. We were never divorced.

Laura (*staring*) What?

Kay Dave never got round to it. So you see, Laura — you didn't miss anything. You wouldn't have been Lady Thursby — I would.

Kevin becomes more agitated

Kevin Laura, this puts a different complexion on things. We have to steady the ship here.

Laura What are you trying to say?

Kay That Dave was a bigamist.

Kevin That's it! We have to keep this absolutely under wraps.

Laura (*faltering*) A bigamist! What does that make me?

Kay A bigamee, I suppose. But I won't say anything if you don't.

Kevin Did you hear that, Laura — we have a compromise.

Kay I only want what I am entitled to.

Laura You're not entitled to anything. (*She clutches the urn closer*)

Kay I am, more than you think. Dave made a will.

Laura What?

Kay After we were married. He was trying to impress me, I suppose. He left me everything, which was nothing then but now ... And didn't you say he hadn't left a will?

Laura But I'm his wife.

Kay We've just established that you're not. Now if my will hasn't been revoked the consequence could be serious ... for you.

Kevin She's in a strong legal position here, Laura.

Laura Will you be quiet, Kevin? Are you suggesting that I don't own anything — not even my house?

Kay I only want my share and if the will hasn't been revoked ...
Laura (*desperately*) Then I revoke it — I revoke it right now.
Kevin Laura, it's not as simple as that.
Laura Isn't it? Then I'll make it simple. (*She advances on Kay*)

Kevin comes between them

Kevin Now, ladies, I'm sure we can sort this out ...
Laura You want your share of him? Well, here it is. (*She hurls the ashes at Kay*)

The ashes spread over Kay and Kevin and on to the floor. There is a cry of shock and horror from the others

And that's all you're getting.
Kevin This is not a solution! (*He manages to wrench the urn from Laura*)

Laura collapses sobbing at the desk. Kevin hands the urn to Jane. He sees the others' appalled gazes. He looks down

My God! Just look. I've got him all over me.
Harvey Now keep calm, Kevin and don't move. Stay exactly where you are. We have Dave to consider. Vi, fetch a brush and dustpan.

Vi exits hurriedly

Kay flicks the ashes off her dress with an expression of distaste

Kay, try to keep it in a neat pile, if you could, we don't want to lose him in the fibres. Not over there, Kev — let's keep it all in one place — brush yourselves over here. Jane, hold the urn ready ...

They struggle to retrieve the ashes

Kevin All I asked was for people to be reasonable. Look at me.
Harvey (*grinning*) I know it's terrible but you must admit, Kev — it's not without its humorous side. Even in death he's still making us laugh.
Kevin It's not funny, Harvey. I'm not laughing and neither is Laura.
Harvey Well, I can understand that. She's just discovered she's the other woman. We'll have to give her time to adjust to the role.

Vi enters with a brush and dustpan. She begins brushing Kay and Kevin down

Jane holds the urn for Vi to return the ashes

Careful. Don't spill any. He's losing weight fast. If we go on like this there won't be enough to spread.

Kay I think I'll go and tidy myself up.

Vi Will you be all right?

Kay Oh, yes. (*She looks across at Laura*) It's not the first time Dave's been all over me.

Kay exits

Laura Did you hear that? Did you see her? She thinks she owns the house already.

Kevin She has a case, Laura. And she's prepared to be reasonable. And I don't think Dave's reputation can take this sort of a battering.

Laura I'm not concerned with his reputation at the moment. Could I lose everything?

Kevin No, you have rights.

Laura I owned three houses — now I have rights!

Harvey You see, the point is, the court may take the view that this is what Dave intended ...

Laura Is that a joke, Harvey?

Harvey It could have been — a joke on you. Did you really know him, Laura? Did any of us really know him? He may have looked back on those days in Cromer as the happiest of his life. And he threw it all away. That's the worst kind of regret — not what destiny chooses for us, that's something we can't help — but when we choose our destiny — and we're wrong.

Laura (*coldly*) Wrong?

Harvey After Cromer, everything may have seemed grey and cold. He may have regretted his ambition — looked back on those sunny days on the sands as the good times — and then looked at you and became bitter. And blamed you. And thought, I'll show her. She's going to get a shock. Wait until Kay pops up with a copy of the will ...

Laura stares incredulously. Harvey's voice dies away

Well, that's what the courts may think ...

Laura So now I'm grey and cold, am I?

Harvey That's not what I think. But what did Dave think? We don't know. He's only just beginning to emerge. It's a voyage of discovery — to find the whole man. And I, for one, find it terribly exciting.
Laura Do you? Well, I don't need a voyage of discovery. I know David. I know he would never have been so underhand.

Kevin gives a harsh laugh

Kevin Wouldn't he?
Laura What does that mean, Kevin?
Kevin Ask Jane if he wouldn't be underhand.
Vi (*hastily*) We don't need to bring Jane into this.
Jane You said you weren't going to mention it anymore.
Kevin I said I'd forgiven you — I didn't say I wouldn't mention it. Why should I be discrete? I begged for discretion — for calm and reasonableness — and I'm covered in ashes!
Jane You can't forgive me because there was nothing to forgive.
Kevin You and Dave — nothing to forgive?
Jane That's right. Because to forgive someone there has to be an offence — and you weren't offended — you weren't even hurt. And if you'd known you wouldn't have done anything about it. You would have gone for a little damage limitation — mended a few fences — anything to keep a client.
Kevin Is that what you were doing in the stationery cupboard? Keeping a client — saving the agency?
Jane Isn't that all you ever cared about? Keeping Dave? You'd have gone into the stationery cupboard yourself if you thought it would have done any good. Perhaps you did. So don't you dare to forgive me. All you ever cared about was your ten per cent of Dave. Well, here it is — you can have it. (*She hurls the ashes into Kevin's face*)
Harvey Oh, no! Not again! (*He snatches the urn from Jane*) Vi, the dustpan! We can't afford to lose anymore. Keep still, Kevin.

Vi and Harvey gather around Kevin, brushing him down

Kevin This is grotesque! I think I've swallowed some.
Jane Well, you've swallowed everything else about Dave — why not his ashes?

Jane exits in tears

Kevin This is revolting! It's up my nose!
Harvey Not the first time he's got up your nose, Kev.
Vi Harvey, can't you see Kevin's upset.

Harvey We'll soon have you cleaned up, Kev.
Kevin I must wash it off! Urgh! (*He breaks free and crosses to the door*)
Laura Kevin!

Kevin stops

What did you mean about David and Jane?
Kevin They made love in a stationery cupboard — in a space no bigger than a hatbox!

Kevin exits into the hall

Harvey and Vi become busy with the urn and dustpan

Laura So they were having an affair.

Harvey and Vi look at each other

Harvey Who?
Laura David and Jane.
Vi (*uneasily*) I wouldn't call it an affair.
Harvey It was on a very small scale — had to be.
Vi And fleeting.
Harvey Brief encounter, really. Thursdays.
Laura Thursdays?
Harvey Stationery cupboard.
Vi Harvey.
Laura How could he?
Harvey Good question. Dave was a many-faceted individual — a man of deep complexity. A genius — a flawed genius, perhaps, but we can't judge him by ordinary standards. He brought so much to the world, Laura. We're still getting hundreds of letters — some from old ladies that would bring tears to your eyes. He brought them warmth and laughter. He reminded them of the times before comedy had to give way to such intellectual programmes as *Does Size Matter?* And makeover programmes so numerous that decorators are creating rock gardens and gardeners are decorating new flats. And those mind-numbing cop shows longer than *The Forsyte Saga* — where it takes half an hour for anyone to speak and two hours before they find the body. And those reality shows. *Boys' Night Out in Ibiza* and how many lagers you can drink before your head blows off! Those old ladies don't want reality — they've had enough in their grim lives — they

50

wanted Dave. Clean, wholesome, family viewing and scripted. It wasn't the real Dave but it was their perception — and that's all that matters. I know Dave wasn't like that — he was a rogue but my God he was a lovable rogue.

Laura Harvey, I knew he was a lovable rogue. I didn't know he was being a lovable rogue with Jane — that he'd been a lovable rogue with Kay. I knew he always had to prove himself — particularly with women. I wasn't a complete fool. I always knew about Vi — that was something I'd learned to accept.

Harvey That's my point — we're still learning about Dave. But what we've learnt doesn't alter —— (*He breaks off*) What was that? (*He stares at Vi*)

Vi's brush strokes become slower

Laura I said I knew about David and Vi but for some reason I was never jealous. Well, I couldn't be — not with Vi.

Harvey Sorry — I didn't quite get that?

Laura But Jane was a complete shock. I thought she was as open as a sunflower. You're right, Harvey. It shows we don't really know anyone. I must say when I heard that, a little iron did enter my soul. I'll never know why he chose Jane. Of course I know why he chose Vi.

Harvey (*more perplexed*) Chose Vi for what?

Laura For an affair. It was to get back at you, Harvey.

Harvey Get back at me? What for?

Laura He was jealous. He'd seen the way you looked at me.

Harvey Looked at you? (*He stares from one to the other*)

Vi keeps busy with the brush and dustpan

Laura The way you flirted.

Harvey Laura — you are the last person I'd flirt with — well, not the last person — yes, the last person. You were married to Dave.

Laura That's not how David saw it. He always suspected you. He blamed you for my coldness. He wouldn't listen to my denials. He always resented you.

Harvey Resented me! Why?

Laura He found you smug and self-assured. In fact he detested you. That time at the pro-am when he ran into your car — that wasn't an accident. He didn't skid on the grass. He saw you showing off to me in your brand new Jag and something snapped. He gave vent to his hatred and put his foot hard down on the accelerator.

Harvey Hatred! I wasn't flirting with you. I was being nice to you. Vi said I should be nice to you.

Laura That wasn't David's perception — and that's why he chose Vi. Why he chose Jane I'll never know ... Or perhaps I do. He may have felt it wasn't really infidelity since he was only unfaithful with plain women.

Harvey stares at Laura, dumbfounded

Now I suppose I'd better see that —— (*She stops herself*) Although I suppose I'd better not call her that. After all, I must see how reasonable she's prepared to be. (*She crosses to the hall door and stops*) Do you realize something? David had laid every woman in this room. My God. And I told her to get back to the chorus. We are the chorus!

Laura exits

Vi I need a drink. (*She crosses to the drinks tray*)
Harvey You and Dave?
Vi Yes.
Harvey When?
Vi When you were covering for him. Remember all that nudging and winking — and if Laura rings we're working late.
Harvey That was you?
Vi Well, not Thursdays — that was when he had a date with the stationery cupboard. I always wondered what he did on Thursdays.
Harvey I never thought for a minute.
Vi Well, you wouldn't would you? As Laura said — you couldn't be jealous of Vi.
Harvey But Dave could have had anyone. Why you?
Vi Why me? Because I was there — like Everest. Isn't that what Dave would have said?
Harvey You know what I mean. Why you? The wife of his closest friend.
Vi Not that close, Harve.
Harvey He wouldn't have done that to me — not without ...
Vi Encouragement?
Harvey Was it because of our friendship? I know you always resented it. Was it your way of getting at me?
Vi I wasn't getting at you. He was getting at you. Laura was right about that — he didn't like you.
Harvey What are you talking about? We were inseparable.
Vi Not inseparable, or it couldn't have happened, could it?
Harvey Why didn't he like me?
Vi I'm not sure. I think it was your swagger — your air of superiority.
Harvey I was never superior.

Vi He thought so. He thought you took too much credit for the show. That you were the puppeteer and he was your puppet.

Harvey He never thought that.

Vi How do you know what he really thought? Didn't you say we never really know anyone, Harve?

Harvey I never gave him that impression.

Vi That was the impression he got. That was his perception ... (*Pause*) This was to be your last series.

Harvey What!

Vi He was letting you go. He was going to prove he could do it without you.

Harvey I see. So he went with you to get at me. What about you? Why did you go with him?

Vi I don't know. I've asked myself that. I suppose I was flattered.

Harvey Flattered! He never flattered you. It was always pull up a couple of chairs and sit down, Vi.

Vi That's why I was flattered.

Harvey You wanted to sleep with the star — that was it, wasn't it? Fame by proxy. After all, who sleeps with the writer?

Vi I do. And I'm too old to be star struck, Harve. I've met famous people before. Do you know what Dave said about fame? He said it means being hated by people you don't even know.

Harvey I never heard him say that.

Vi He said it to me.

Harvey I still can't believe it.

Vi You're a comedy writer. You never could face reality. You won't even watch the six o'clock news — you can barely face the weather forecast. (*She looks into the urn*) Do you think we've got enough?

Harvey And where did all this take place? Did you find a cupboard somewhere — or the back of a car — or under a hedge?

Vi He came to the house.

Harvey stares at Vi in astonishment

Harvey (*in awed tones*) Dave came to my house?

Vi Yes.

Harvey What did he think of it?

Vi He admired our taste.

Harvey Really? (*He considers this for a moment*)

Vi And that wasn't all he admired ... Surprised? "Pull up a couple of chairs and sit down, Vi." Remember how you'd laugh — well, you're not laughing now. (*She holds up the dustpan*) That's all I can find.

Harvey holds out the urn. Vi drops the ashes in. They regard each other for a moment.

You're not going to throw them in my face, are you?
Harvey No. Dave can't spare them. I'll see if I can salvage any from Kevin — he must have had a couple of ounces down his shirt front ...

Harvey exits into the hall with the urn, brush and dustpan

Jane enters from the garden

Sound of voices off

Jane They're assembling on the bottom lawn for the spreading of the ashes.
Vi We haven't got much to spread.
Jane Sorry about that. I just got ...
Vi I know. Sometimes you just feel like throwing ashes. Where's Laura?
Jane Down the bottom of the garden. Arm in arm with Kay.
Vi What!
Jane I must say she's a great one for picking herself up. Apparently they've both agreed to be reasonable. Kevin will be pleased. Fences mended — damage limited.
Vi I'm sorry.
Jane Laura asked if you and Harvey would carry the urn down for the ceremony.
Vi (*staring*) Why us?
Jane Because you're his oldest friends. She thought it would be appropriate.

Vi chuckles

Jane Why are you laughing?
Vi You don't know how funny that is.
Jane She doesn't want it funny — she wants it solemn. She said if you could manage a sort of slow walk.
Vi A slow walk! After all that's happened I can barely stagger.
Jane And then hand the urn to the vicar with due reverence.
Vi Due reverence! She doesn't want me to curtsy, does she? Well, there's one thing about Laura — she doesn't bear a grudge.
Jane Oh, I don't know. I was to have carried the urn. She obviously changed her mind — after what happened. Still, at least she's speaking to me.

Vi Why shouldn't she? She speaks to me.
Jane Why shouldn't she speak to you?
Vi Why do you think?

Jane stares at Vi for a moment. She puts a hand to her mouth

Jane You don't mean ... Not you as well?
Vi Yes.
Jane I didn't know about you.
Vi I didn't know about you. Dave could certainly keep a secret when he wanted to.
Jane I still don't know why. Why did we do it? What were we looking for?
Vi Approval.
Jane Approval? Was that what it was?
Vi That's how Dave worked. It's what we all wanted. Dave knew that. He'd find a weakness and exploit it. Have you noticed something? In spite of all that's happened a maidenly blush has never crossed your cheek and Kevin hasn't stammered. Only Dave could make you do that.
Jane (*pause*) You know, he wasn't really a very nice person, was he?
Vi No.
Jane Do you think Laura sought his approval?
Vi No — nothing could shatter Laura's self-esteem. I think that's why Dave married her. But there would have been others.
Jane Do you think so?
Vi There's seven days in a week and only two of us. There must have been more.
Jane I thought that woman from make-up looked very distressed at the funeral.
Vi And what about the casting lady — she was drenched in tears.

Jane and Vi begin to laugh

Jane Funny — you'd think it would make me feel worse but it doesn't.
Vi A trouble shared ...

Jane and Vi embrace

Harvey enters from the hall carrying the urn

Jane gives Vi a quick kiss on the cheek

Jane I'll see you down there ... (*She gives Harvey a nervous glance*)

Jane exits into the garden

Harvey You told her, didn't you?
Vi Yes.
Harvey Why?
Vi I thought it would make her feel better.
Harvey What about my feelings?
Vi (*studying Harvey*) What about them?

Harvey looks into the urn

Harvey I just hope we've got enough. (*He sighs*) Why couldn't she have buried the urn — then it wouldn't have mattered.
Vi She considered that. Then she thought about Bruno. She didn't want the dog digging him up.
Harvey What! (*He grins despite himself*)
Vi She didn't want that to happen.
Harvey No. Then we'll just have to make the best of things.
Vi What about Kevin?
Harvey I was too late. He'd flushed him down the loo.
Vi Poor Dave. That's awful.
Harvey I think Kevin quite enjoyed it. So I had to improvise.

Vi peers in the urn

Vi You must have done. He's certainly put on weight since I saw him last.
Harvey I emptied the ashtrays.
Vi I can see that. There's a cigarette end. (*She removes a cigarette end from the urn*)
Harvey Good thing they didn't see that.
Vi Well, he was a heavy smoker. (*She looks into the urn again*) There's something else. He's changed colour.
Harvey Do you think so?
Vi He's browner. There's something else in there.
Harvey Yes.
Vi What is it?
Harvey Muesli.
Vi Muesli!
Harvey I told you — I had to improvise. It's all I could find in the kitchen. Look, I didn't spill those ashes!

Vi starts to giggle

Vi You mean we're spreading muesli?
Harvey It's only symbolic, isn't it?
Vi I hope it's organic.

Harvey starts to smile. The sound of "Getting to Know You" booms out from the garden. Vi and Harvey laugh

Vi We have to be serious. As Dave's oldest friends we're expected to process down the garden bearing the urn — then hand it with due reverence to the vicar. She wants us to walk ... sort of slowly.
Harvey As if we were getting married?
Vi I suppose so — in step, I imagine.
Harvey Jointly holding the ...
Vi Yes ...

Harvey and Vi tentatively each take a handle of the urn. They start to move off. Vi stops

Harvey What's the matter?
Vi I feel as if I've just won the mixed doubles at Wimbledon. What do you feel?
Harvey I feel it's a strange way to spread muesli.

Vi smiles

Vi I just hope Bruno doesn't grab your leg ——

Harvey kisses Vi on the lips

   Why did you do that?
Harvey I don't know.
Vi You're not still following Dave?
Harvey No. (*Pause*) Now I know what he meant by love and laughter. He loved you and laughed at me. I think I hate him.
Vi That was his ... perception.
Harvey But he was right about one thing. Laughter does help to bind wounds ...

Harvey and Vi start to move off again. Harvey stops

   I don't think I'll write that book.

Vi I wouldn't.
Harvey I might make a start on the play.
Vi That's a good idea.
Harvey I think I'll call it ... "Wife After Death".
Vi They won't get it ...
Harvey I thought you might ...

The music swells louder

Vi and Harvey attempt a solemn exit and trip on the step. They spill the ashes once more ...

CURTAIN

FURNITURE AND PROPERTY LIST

ACT I

On stage: Door
French windows (open) with curtains half drawn
Desk. *On it*: paper, pen
Sofa
Chairs
Sideboard
Drinks tray. *On it*: drinks, glasses
Stand. *On it*: open coffin
Bin

Personal: **Kevin**: dark glasses, handkerchief, notes (in pocket)
Harvey: notes (in pocket)

ACT II

Strike: Coffin

Set: Brass urn with handles containing ashes (on sideboard)
Open curtains on french windows

Off stage: Paper, photograph (**Kay**)
Brush, dustpan (**Vi**)
Cigarette end (in urn) (**Harvey**)

LIGHTING PLOT

ACT I

To open: Interior lighting with curtains half-drawn. Spotlight on coffin

Cue 1	**Harvey** switches off the light	(Page 2)
	Take out spotlight	

ACT II

To open: Dull interior lighting. Spotlight on urn

No cues

EFFECTS PLOT

Please see the note on page 61 regarding the use of copyright material.

ACT I

Cue 1   To open   (Page 1)
           "Getting to Know You" from The King and I
           plays faintly

ACT II

Cue 2   **Harvey** starts to smile   (Page 56)
           "Getting to Know You" booms out from the garden

Cue 3   **Harvey**: "I thought you might ..."   (Page 57)
           Music swells louder

MUSIC USE NOTE

Licensees are solely responsible for obtaining formal written permission from copyright owners to use copyrighted music in the performance of this play and are strongly cautioned to do so. If no such permission is obtained by the licensee, then the licensee must use only original music that the licensee owns and controls. Licensees are solely responsible and liable for all music clearances and shall indemnify the copyright owners of the play(s) and their licensing agent, Samuel French, against any costs, expenses, losses and liabilities arising from the use of music by licensees. Please contact the appropriate music licensing authority in your territory for the rights to any incidental music.

IMPORTANT BILLING AND CREDIT REQUIREMENTS

If you have obtained performance rights to this title, please refer to your licensing agreement for important billing and credit requirements.